Magic

SECRETS OF THE SUPERNATURAL

Magic

R E B E C C A   S T E F O F F

Marshall Cavendish
Benchmark
New York

Marshall Cavendish Benchmark
99 White Plains Road
Tarrytown, New York 10591-9001
www.marshallcavendish.us

Library of Congress Cataloging-in-Publication Data
Stefoff, Rebecca
Magic / by Rebecca Stefoff.
p. cm. — (Secrets of the supernatural)
Summary: "A critical exploration of magic, its history, and practitioners" —Provided by publisher.
Includes bibliographical references and index.
ISBN: 978-0-7614-2636-3
1. Magic. I. Title. II. Series
BF1611.S7963 2007
133.4´3—dc22
2007006722

Editor: Joyce Stanton
Publisher: Michelle Bisson
Art Director: Anahid Hamparian
Series Designer: Anne Scatto / PIXEL PRESS

Images provided by Rose Corbett Gordon, Art Editor, Mystic, CT, from the following sources:
Cover: Hulton Archive/Getty Images; *back cover:* Nancy Richmond/The Image Works; *pages 1, 33, 35, 37, 64:*
Charles Walker/Topfoto/The Image Works; *page 2:* Victoria & Albert Museum/Art Resource, NY; *page 6:*
Sandro Vannini/Corbis; *pages 8, 9:* Hulton Archive/Getty Images; *page 10 top, 77:* Time & Life Pictures/Getty
Images; *page 10 bottom:* Scott Smith/Corbis; *page 11:* Print Collector/HIP/The Image Works; *pages 12, 54:*
Ann Ronan Picture Library/HIP/Art Resource, NY; *page 14:* Edward Frederick Brewtnaall/Bridgeman Art
Library/Getty Images; *page 15:* Jo McChesney/Getty Images; *page 18:* Ted Spiegel/Corbis; *page 20:* William
Bloomhuff/Taxi/Getty Images; *page 22:* Scherl/SV-Bilderdienst/The Image Works; *page 23:* Jeri Gleiter/
Taxi/Getty Images; *pages 24, 25:* Werner Forman/Art Resource, NY; *page 26:* Olivier Martel/Corbis; *page 27:*
Reuters/Corbis; *pages 28, 78:* AAAC/Topham/The Image Works; *page 30:* Erik Dreyer/Stone/Getty; *pages 36,
69:* Topham/The Image Works; *page 38:* Jeff Greenberg/The Image Works; *page 40:* Maurice Branger/Roger-
Viollet/The Image Works; *page 42:* British Library/HIP/Art Resource, NY; *page 43:* FA/Roger-Viollet/The Image
Works; *pages 45, 72, 74, 76:* Mary Evans Picture Library/The Image Works; *page 46:* Private Collection/
Bridgeman Art Library; *page 48:* DPA/RV/The Image Works; *page 50:* Alinari Archives/The Image Works;
page 53: Roger-Viollet/The Image Works; *page 56:* Giraudon/Art Resource, NY; *page 58:* Erich Lessing/Art
Resource, NY *pages 61, 70:* SuperStock; *pages 63, 66:* Scala/Art Resource, NY; *page 65:* Art Resource, NY;
page 67: Beinecke Rare Book and Manuscript Library, Yale University; *page 80:* Bettmann/Corbis.

Printed in Malaysia

1   3   5   6   4   2

FRONT COVER: Boris Karloff starred in *The Mummy* (1932), a tale
of Egyptian sorcery.
BACK COVER: In magical lore, a broken mirror is a sign of bad
luck to come.
HALF TITLE: A grimoire, or book of spells, rests on an altar used for
magical practices.
TITLE PAGE: The sorceress Nimue prepares to cast a spell on Merlin,
the legendary wizard.

Contents

The eyes of the long-dead pharaoh Tutankhamen seem almost alive in this magnificent golden funeral mask. Its discovery sparked rumors about the magical powers of the ancient Eygptians.

Is It True?

"DEATH COMES ON WINGS TO HE WHO ENTERS
THE TOMB OF A PHARAOH."

"Can you see anything?" Lord Carnarvon's voice trembled with excitement.

Howard Carter was almost too dazed to answer. He stood as if in a trance, gazing through a small hole in a stone wall. He'd chiseled the hole and shoved a candle through it so that he could glimpse the room on the other side. "As my eyes grew accustomed to the light," he later wrote, "details of the room within emerged slowly from the mist, strange animals, statues, and gold—everywhere the glint of gold."

Then came Carnarvon's hopeful, anxious question: "Can you see anything?"

"Yes," Carter replied, "wonderful things."

It was November 26, 1922, and the two men stood in a narrow stone passageway sixteen steps below the surface of the Valley of the Kings in Egypt. With them was Evelyn Herbert, Lord Carnarvon's daughter. They were almost unbearably excited, because they suspected that the chamber on the other side of the stone wall was the entrance to the tomb of Tutankhamen, a pharaoh who had ruled ancient Egypt and died more than three thousand years before. Carter had been searching for

With his daughter Evelyn, Lord Carnarvon was one of the first people to enter Tutankhamen's tomb.

Tutankhamen's burial site for six years, funded by Carnarvon. At last, he believed, he had found it, and now the three were about to become the first people in modern times to open the tomb and enter the pharaoh's final resting place.

They spent hours in the numerous rooms of the tomb, awed by the importance of their discovery, dazzled by the treasures heaped all around. The place was magnificent—and eerie. Things seemed to move in the flickering lantern light. Carter noticed three large couches carved in the form of monstrous animals. With "their heads throwing grotesque shadows on the wall behind them," he later wrote, "they were almost terrifying."

At last the discoverers left the tomb, overwhelmed by what they had seen. Carter resealed the entry and assigned men to guard the passageway night and day. The tomb would not be officially opened until a full team of scientists and scholars, along with representatives of the Egyptian government, could be present.

Under Carter's orders, laboratories and photographic darkrooms were set up *in the desert. A stream of archae-ological experts from many coun-tries came to the Valley of the Kings to take part in the excava-tion. The Metropolitan Museum of Art in New York City sent a photographer to capture the historic event in pictures and on film. As the scientists and schol-ars settled into tents in the val-ley, they rubbed elbows with a growing flock of reporters who filed colorful—and sometimes highly imaginative—newspaper stories of each day's findings.*

By now, the world was fasci-nated with Carter's discovery. Talk of the excavation was on everybody's lips. What ancient secrets might be contained in the

Carter posted guards in the pas-sageway to the tomb to prevent robbery—something the ancient Egyptians had also feared.

pharaoh's tomb? Would Tutankhamen's mummy still be there? Along with the eager questions were a few fearful mutterings: Might not open-ing the tomb and disturbing the dead have evil consequences? Perhaps ancient Egyptian magicians had placed a curse on the tomb to protect the pharaoh and his treasures. . . .

It took almost two months for Carter and the others to clear a path through the tomb. In order to make a permanent record of the excavation, every object in every room had to be photographed and sketched in place before it could be removed for detailed study. Finally, on February 17, 1923, Carter was ready for what he called

The treasures buried with the pharaoh were meant to accompany him into the afterlife. Instead, they were destined for modern museums.

the most important moment of the entire excavation: the opening of the inner burial chamber, which would likely contain the pharaoh's mummy. Carnarvon invited scholars and officials to watch as the entrance to the special chamber was unsealed. As Carter led the observers inside, they beheld a huge golden shrine. A set of doors protected it. Would Tutankhamen's mummified body lie behind them?

It was a stupendous moment. And a frustrating one—for everyone would have to wait weeks before the doors could be opened. The archaeologists had decided it was necessary to pay attention to the tomb's other artifacts, many of which were made of wood and cloth and were falling to bits and were in urgent need of preservation. So Carter, still not knowing for sure if King Tut's remains were actually there, reluctantly postponed his investigation of the shrine and set about caring for the other treasures.

The archaeologists and their helpers went about their work. Then, two or three weeks later, something happened. It was a small event, hardly noticeable: A mosquito bit Lord Carnarvon on the cheek.

How bad can a single mosquito bite be?

The bite got infected. Some versions of the story say that Carnarvon's servant accidentally nicked it while shaving his master, but maybe the earl simply scratched the bite. At any rate, the infection was serious. When news that Carnarvon was ill reached the world, at least one person was sure she knew the cause. Marie Corelli, a popular English novelist who was interested in supernatural subjects, wrote a letter that was published in newspapers in London and New York. She said:

I cannot but think some risks are run by breaking into the last rest of a king in Egypt whose tomb is specially and solemnly guarded, and robbing him of his possessions. According to a rare book I possess, which is not in the British Museum, entitled *The Egyptian History of the Pyramids*, the most dire punishment follows any rash intruder into a sealed tomb. The book . . . names 'secret poisons enclosed in boxes in such wise that those who touch them shall not know how they come to suffer'. That is why I ask, Was it a mosquito bite that has so seriously infected Lord Carnarvon?

Novelist Marie Corelli claimed to know of an ancient Egyptian curse.

Corelli went on to repeat a warning from the book: "Death comes on wings to he who enters the tomb of a pharaoh."

Carnarvon's condition went from bad to worse. He developed pneumonia, a serious illness of the lungs. On April 5, about two weeks after Corelli's letter appeared and less than two months after the opening of the burial chamber, Lord Carnarvon died in a hospital in Cairo, Egypt.

The lights went out in Cairo when Carnarvon died, and darkness spread over the city. Back on Carnarvon's English estate, according to his son, the earl's dog Susie howled at the exact moment of her master's death. This, it seemed, was no ordinary death. The mummy's curse had struck down the man who had paid for the digging-up of the tomb!

The newspapers jumped on the story of an ancient magic that had reached across three thousand years to kill an English nobleman. Soon the papers would be reporting other deaths said to have been brought about by the "Curse of King Tutankhamen." . . .

Magic hadn't protected Tutankhamen's tomb from being opened— but had an ancient spell really worked vengeance on those who opened it? In the early years of the twentieth century, such an idea seemed outlandish. Sir Henry Rider Haggard, the author of *She* and other adventure novels with supernatural elements,

thought that magic was pure fiction. He called the idea of a curse on Tut's tomb "dangerous" nonsense that fueled people's superstitions. But not everyone agreed with him.

Sir Arthur Conan Doyle, another English writer, was

Sir Arthur Conan Doyle, the creator of Sherlock Holmes, would not rule out supernatural causes for Carnarvon's death. Doyle believed in ghosts, fairies, and magic.

trained as a doctor and invented one of the world's most famous symbols of reason, the detective Sherlock Holmes. Yet Doyle believed in the supernatural. He suggested that Carnarvon had been killed by "elementals," powerful magical forces set in place by Tutankhamen's priest-magicians.

In the three thousand years between the sealing of King Tut's tomb and its opening, magic had only partly lost its hold on people's minds. Nearly one hundred years after the opening of Tutankhamen's tomb, the subject of magic continues to fascinate believers and nonbelievers alike.

What Is Magic?

When you hear the word *magic*, what comes into your mind? Do you think of marvels and enchantments, stories about talking animals that offer three wishes, or princesses cast into deep sleep by spells? Do your thoughts turn to strange, thrilling powers and wand-waving wizards? Perhaps you think of darker magic—scary, mysterious forces, like the curse that some people believed killed Lord Carnarvon in Egypt.

Or maybe you think of card tricks, or rabbits being pulled out of hats. That's performance magic, or stage magic. Skilled performance magicians do things that seem impossible, from the ever-popular stunt of sawing someone in half to making a diamond ring disappear and then reappear in someone else's pocket on the other side of the room. This kind of magic is also called illusionism. The magic of a good performer's act is an illusion—something that isn't what it appears to be.

Illusionists use ingenuity, psychology, and a great deal of skill

An enchanted princess sleeps for a century in the tale known as "Sleeping Beauty."

and practice to create their effects. In the past, some of these artists claimed to have hidden knowledge, or occult powers. In modern times, though, very few illusionists seriously claim to practice "real" magic. Their admiring audiences know that what looks like magic is actually a clever, well-done trick. Occult magic, the spells-and-wizards kind, however, is based on the belief that certain people *can* harness supernatural powers. Today some people who claim to practice occult magic use the term *magick* to separate it from illusionism.

People didn't always draw a clear line between the two kinds of magic. At times when being an occult magician was dangerous, because people thought it meant you worked with demons, performing a clever trick could get you into trouble. That's what happened to one young woman in the early seventeenth century. She amazed a group of nobles with a trick that is familiar to many illusionists today. First, she tore a napkin into pieces. Then she produced what seemed to be the same napkin, only it was whole and untorn. The young illusionist was hauled off to face the Inquisition, the arm of the Roman Catholic Church that dealt harshly with crimes against the faith, including witchcraft. She was lucky—she was only cast out of the church.

Occult magic is the ability to control people and events (or at least influence them a little) in ways that can't be explained by everyday experience or by science. A magician can step outside the world of the ordinary to perform extraordinary feats. But as you will see in this book, people who have studied magic over the

To cut someone into pieces, an illusionist relies on mirrors and hidden compartments, not magical powers.

ages have had many different ideas about what magic is and how to do it.

Can Magic Be Tested?

Becoming invisible, flying, conjuring up spirits and visions, turning people into toads, bringing the dead back to life, controlling the weather, making people fall in (or out of) love—these are just a few of the extraordinary things that magicians have been said to do. But is there any way to test these remarkable claims?

Skeptics would say that magic doesn't exist . . . or at least that it hasn't been proven. A skeptic is someone who uses a tool called critical thinking to examine all kinds of claims. Thinking critically means probing below the surface and not taking anything for granted. It means asking questions like: Who says so? What is the evidence? How reliable is that evidence? Is there another way to explain the facts that is just as likely to be true, or even more likely to be true? And can the claim be tested, such as through experiments?

Magic doesn't hold up very well to critical thinking. For one thing, magic is often performed in secrecy. Most magicians, past and present, have been unwilling to perform in front of audiences, especially skeptical audiences. Some of them say, in fact, that magic won't work in the presence of a skeptic. Of course, this means that magic can never be scientifically examined.

Failed Magic

According to believers, there are many reasons why magic can fail besides the presence of a skeptic. Take the example of a magician who performs a ritual to bring rain. One traditional Chinese rain ritual involved burning a mixture of dried herbs while walking through a pattern of lines drawn on the ground and speaking the words of a spell. If the magician performed the ritual and it rained a few days later, maybe even a week later, people would be certain that the ritual had brought the rain. But if the magician performed the ritual and it didn't rain for a long time, it would be easy to think that the magician had just made a mistake in the ritual. (Some skeptics have suggested that this is why so many magical ceremonies and spells are rather complicated. If the magic doesn't do anything, the explanation is simple: The magician got one of the words wrong, or used the wrong ingredient in a potion.) Countermagic, or magic working against magic, could also explain why the ritual failed to work. This would mean that a rival magician performed a ritual to keep the first magician from succeeding.

Another explanation for failed magic is that the magician's will was not strong enough, or his or her mind was not properly focused. This makes working magic different from science, chemistry, or even cooking. The unique individual element—the strength of the magician's mind and will—is all-important in magic. A cook can follow a recipe and bake pretty much identical cakes on a hundred different occasions, even if he or she is watching television in the kitchen, or thinking about other things. But a magician, it's said, cannot perform magic unless his or her entire mind is fully concentrated, which is a difficult task.

The importance of the magician's will puts magic beyond the realm of proof or disproof. If a spell or ritual has no effect, a believer says that the fault lies in the magician, not in magic itself. Christine Wicker, a journalist who investigated magic in modern

A Native American shaman concentrates on the symbols he creates as part of a ritual to bring rain. The full ritual takes four days.

America, met one believer who told her, "Magic will never be proved."

Magical beliefs and practices may lack proof, but they have been part of human life since before the beginning of written history. Tales of magical deeds fill us with curiosity, wonder, fear—and a little envy, too. Who hasn't dreamed of having secret powers over the world around us, or being able to influence people at a distance? In the pages that follow, you'll sit in on magical ceremonies, meet famous wizards, and discover some of the ways people have explained magic. You'll also learn more about the deadly curse of King Tut, so that you can decide for yourself whether or not it is true.

In some traditional cultures, shamans act as bridges between
the natural and supernatural worlds. Filled with mystical power,
the shaman's hand may heal with a touch.

Ancient Mysteries

A "mood of terror" came over Knud Rasmussen during the eeriest part of the ritual. A sorcerer had just said that the spirits of the dead were standing right there in the room!

Rasmussen was a Greenlander. His father was Danish, and his mother was a woman of the Inuit, once called Eskimos, the native people of Greenland. It was the early part of the twentieth century, and Rasmussen was studying Inuit customs and beliefs, traveling to remote settlements on the huge, ice-covered island. On the night when the spirits entered the room, he was at a magic ceremony in an Inuit village.

The Shaman and the Storm

It was the third evening of a terrible blizzard. No one in the village had been able to hunt for several days. A shaman or sorcerer, Rasmussen learned, was going to try to calm the storm using traditional magic. Rasmussen's hosts offered to escort him to the ceremony, which would take place in a large igloo owned by a man named Kingiuna.

Knud Rasmussen, pictured here, witnessed a powerful battle between a shaman and a storm.

"The storm seemed now to have reached its peak," Rasmussen wrote. The winds were so violent that he could hardly walk. "We were all armed with large snow knives and thrust our way with faces bowed close to the ice towards the little village in which the ceremony was to be held." Rasmussen was told that the storm was the crying of Narsuk, an infant giant who lived in the sky. The shaman would try to find out why Narsuk was angry and then try to "tame" the storm.

The igloo was warm, lit by lanterns and crowded with men, women, children, and dogs. Everyone feasted on dried salmon, blubber, and frozen seal carcasses, so cold that the diners had to blow on the food before eating so that they wouldn't tear the skin from their lips and tongues. It was the last of the meat. If the people couldn't hunt tomorrow, they would go hungry.

"The shaman of the evening," Rasmussen wrote, "was Hoqarnaq, a young man with intelligent eyes and swift movements." Hoqarnaq explained to Rasmussen that he had only a few spirits to help him. There was his dead father, who had become an evil spirit since his death, and his father's helping spirit, a giant troll with fingernails long enough to pierce through a man's body. Another spirit was a figure Hoqarnaq had made of snow that came when he called it. The final spirit was a red stone Hoqarnaq had found when hunting. It was shaped like a head. Hoqarnaq had killed a reindeer close to where he found the stone, then wrapped the stone in a headband made of the reindeer's skin. This made the stone-spirit into a magician, doubling its power.

To perform the ritual, Hoqarnaq would have to summon these spirits. But he could not do it, he said—it was beyond his strength. The women crowded around, encouraging and praising him. Hoqarnaq repeated, "It is a difficult thing to speak the truth, it is a difficult thing to conjure up hidden forces."

After many protests, Hoqarnaq finally went slowly into a trance. Before, he had looked very tired, with drooping eyelids, but suddenly he opened his eyes with a wild look and made a gurgling sound. A spirit had entered him.

Hoqarnaq began dancing and leaping. Then he described two spirits that he saw standing in the igloo. When the people finally recognized the descriptions, the mood of terror fell upon everyone. The descriptions belonged to a man and woman who had died very recently. "[T]hese two people were moving among them only a few days ago," Rasmussen said. "Now they have become evil spirits which call up storm and tempest."

Suddenly Hoqarnaq seized Kingiuna, the host, by the

Did the spirits of the dead visit that lantern-lit igloo where Rasmussen watched? His companions believed they did.

throat and shook him violently. Kingiuna gasped, groaned, and struggled, but finally he fell silent. Then he started whispering and obeying Hoqarnaq's orders. The shaman dragged Kingiuna around inside the igloo until Kingiuna seemed to be dead. Hoqarnaq was killing the storm, with Kingiuna as the effigy, or representation, of the storm. Hoqarnaq gripped the seemingly lifeless body, bit Kingiuna hard in the neck, shook him "to and fro like a dog that has overcome its opponent," and finally dropped him onto the floor.

After dancing for a few moments, the magician knelt next to Kingiuna's body. Slowly, he massaged it back to life. Kingiuna stood up. The two men repeated the ritual—dance, death, and return to life—until Kingiuna had been killed three times in all.

Rasmussen understood the meaning of these acts: "Man has to demonstrate his superiority over the storm."

When Kingiuna came back to life for the third time, Hoqarnaq collapsed on the floor. Now Kingiuna was in a trance. He had become the sorcerer! Kingiuna said he saw the spirits of naked men and women flying through the air, unleashing blizzards. Narsuk, the giant child, was "shattering the lungs of the air with his weeping." One air spirit was especially frightening, said Kingiuna. He was full

An Inuit carving shows a shaman in a trance, attended by two helping spirits in the form of small animal-like creatures.

of holes, and the wind whistled through them. Kingiuna asked the crowd of waiting women and men, "Do you see the spirits, the storm, the gale that roars past overhead with the rushing of great birds' wings?"

Hoqarnaq got up from the floor. Together the two men sang to a powerful, protective spirit called the Mother of the Sea Creatures:

Mother, great Mother in the depths!
Take it, take evil away from us.
Come, come, spirit of the deeps!
One of your earth-children is calling
  to you.
Bite the enemy to death!
Come, come, spirit of the deeps!

Another carved Inuit shaman seems to dance. Dancing is an important part of many magical rituals.

Everyone in the igloo joined in the singing. And now everyone seemed to see the flying spirits, "the hordes of the fleeing dead," and hear the giant wings. Rasmussen said that "it is as though the whole of nature has come to life around us."

The singing ended. The battle was over. With the aid of the helping spirits, Hoqarnaq and Kingiuna had fought the storm and won. They told everyone to go home, even though the wind still raged outside the igloo. The next day, they said, would bring fine weather. "And sure enough," wrote Rasmussen, "the following day we travelled on in dazzling sunshine over snow blown firm by the wind."

Roots of Magic

People like Hoqarnaq were the first magicians. Anthropologists (scholars who study human cultures) have found evidence of them in nearly all societies. They still exist in Tibet, Brazil, and other places where people can be found living in traditional ways. Known as shamans, sorcerers, medicine men and women, or witch

doctors, they are believed to have special powers.

The shaman's most important power is the ability to communicate with the spirit world, usually in visions, dreams, or trances. This makes the shaman a link between the community of the living and the supernatural realm inhabited by gods, demons, the dead, and nature spirits.

Shamans have had many roles. Healing is one of their most important duties. They

In Senegal, West Africa, a medicine man sprays a girl with water that is believed to give her some of his own spiritual or magical power.

call on the spirits to help their patients, but many of them also possess great practical knowledge, such as the use of herbal medicines to cure illness and care for wounds. Another important duty concerns the food supply. Shamans are in charge of sacrifices and other rituals to bring good hunting and good crops. They also perform divination, asking the spirits to answer questions or reveal the future. At times of birth and death, they guide souls into and out of the world. Often shamans are the lore keepers of their people, carrying songs, stories, and histories in their memories.

The origins of shamans are hidden in the mists of time.

A woman shaman in Siberia. Her neighbors believe she can cause or cure disease, lift curses, and explain mysteries.

Some anthropologists, though, think that the earliest known images of shamans and magic are found on the walls of caves in Europe and North Africa. These pictures, painted tens of thousands of years ago—before written history—by our Stone Age ancestors, include a few scenes that can be interpreted as shamans performing hunting magic. Human figures with antlers, or the heads of birds, or the paws of bears, are painted next to images of the animals that were hunted. Some anthropologists think that these figures

Hunters or warriors? Although we cannot know the full meaning of these 8,000-year-old figures on a Spanish cave wall, some experts think that prehistoric cave paintings had magical significance for our ancestors who created them.

resemble the costumes made of animal parts that certain shamans still wear when performing hunting magic. A cave painting at Lascaux, in France, even seems to show a staff or wand, topped with the figure of a bird, next to the man who might be a shaman.

No one can really know the meaning of the prehistoric cave paintings. Modern scholars interpret them in many different ways. But by the time people started writing down their history and beliefs, magic was well established in many parts of the world. Records of all kinds of ancient magic have been preserved. There are Near Eastern spells to protect houses from harmful spirits and to bring easy childbirth, Chinese charts for fortune-telling, sacred texts that Tibetans wore as charms to defend themselves from evil magic, and more.

Today, in an age shaped by science and technology, it is easy to overlook the importance that people have placed on magic throughout history. Some modern scholars, however, have called magic the "third current" of civilization, as influential in human societies as religion and science. (In some societies, magic and religion have been closely linked.)

Magic has given people a way to explain the world around them: the crops that fail, the winds that blow, sickness that comes and goes, and the fact that some people enjoy good fortune while others suffer misfortune. Magic offers more than explanations, though. It also offers the promise of power—to those who can master it.

Does someone feel a sudden, stabbing pain as the needle is driven into this doll? For ages people have tried to bring harm to their enemies through the magical use of dolls and figurines.

The Power of Magic

B lack and white. High and low. Private and public. People have come up with many labels and categories for magic. No single definition, and no one set of labels, can contain the whole sprawling subject of magic. Yet magical belief rests on a couple of key ideas about how the universe works. These principles support a vast and varied array of magical practices.

Principles of Magic

The central principle of magic is correspondence, which means that two things agree with each other, or correspond to each other, and are connected by invisible links that don't follow the everyday laws of cause and effect. These hidden links are the means by which magic is believed to work.

"Voodoo dolls" are an example of how a magical link works. A voodoo doll is a small statue or figurine made to represent the person who is the target of the magic. In a sense, the doll *becomes* the person when it is activated by magic—by the right spell being said over it, perhaps, or by the magical power within the person who made it. The doll is believed to be magically linked to the person who is meant to suffer harm, so that whatever is done to the doll will be suffered by the person. A pin stuck in the doll's leg, for example, is supposed to make the person feel pain in that leg. A speck of gold pressed into the doll's hand would bring money to the person because of the magical correspondence between the doll and the person.

The term *voodoo doll* comes from voodoo, or Vodou, an African-Caribbean religion with many magical elements, but such figures have been used all over the world, for thousands of years. Magical spells on ancient clay tablets from Mesopotamia (modern Iraq) mention figurines made for sorcery. In traditional Russian magic, a magician might knot a few stalks of grain in a field into the shape of a doll, causing harm (it was thought) to the person who would later harvest the grain.

Magical correspondence takes several forms. In imitative magic, the magical action is performed on a symbol that copies the real target in some way. The Russian grain doll is an example of imitative magic. So is a voodoo doll, if it is simply a figure made of wax, or clay, or some other material. But if the doll includes something from the target's body, such as a strand of hair, or even a ribbon or button or scrap of cloth that the target once wore, it becomes an example of sympathetic magic.

Sympathy in magic means a thread of connection that links things that were once joined, even if they are separated by space or time. Some magicians think that sympathetic magic is the most powerful kind of magic because that thread of connection links the target's soul, or essence, with the magical tool. Aleister Crowley, a twentieth-century magician, took precautions to keep anyone from getting hold of his hair or fingernail clippings, because he was afraid that these cast-off bits of his body could be used to attack him magically.

But sympathetic magic can work for good as well as for harm. In ancient Egypt, for example, carved stone pillars called *cippi* stood in public places. They were covered with spells against all kinds of dangerous things, from venomous animals such as scorpions to destructive demons. People poured water over the *cippi*. As the water came into contact with the sacred stone, it absorbed the stone's magical power. After that, people could collect the water and carry it around with them for healing and protection.

In one of his books, modern magician Aleister Crowley was portrayed in a yoga pose.

Another principle of magic is summed up in the words *As above, so below*. This magical formula is closely related to astrology, the branch of magic that deals with answering questions and predicting the future by studying the movements of the heavenly bodies. *As above, so below* may have come down through the ages from the ancient city of Babylon, in Mesopotamia, where magic and astrology were practiced. It means that things in the universe (above) are mirrored on Earth (below). By looking to the stars and planets, the astrologer could see what was happening, or what was going to happen, in the human world.

As above, so below goes beyond astrology. It applies to magic in general. In the magical view, small things correspond to large things (like a doll to a person). Everything that happens in the real world of sights and sounds is connected to things that exist on a higher, invisible plane. The key to magic is turning the formula around, so that it becomes *As below, so above.* This means that a magical action taken on the lower level—such as wearing an amulet for good luck, or whispering a love spell over a photograph—makes something happen on the higher level. A magician can manipulate words and symbols to influence the world, or even the universe.

The Magician's Power

In most magical traditions, magicians were made, not born. While some people might have been born with a gift for magic, they still needed training in order to control the gift and reach their full powers. A magician-in-training could be a shaman's apprentice, or an assistant to the village wisewoman or "white witch," who knew the lore of herbs and spells. Sometimes magic was a family affair. Elders proficient in the arts would pass their knowledge—and their responsibilities—on to younger members of their families. More formal studies were undertaken by pupils of advanced magicians, or scholars of magic.

Another way to learn magic was simply to study on one's own. This was a common route to becoming a magician in Europe after about 1300, as more magical texts became available. Some of these texts were philosophical works on the theory of magic. Others were practical handbooks called grimoires, collections of spells and rituals.

Learning is only part of what makes a magician. A magician also needs power, the ability to turn his or her learning into magical actions. What is the source of a magician's power? Even magicians themselves have not agreed on the answer to that question.

There are three main theories about magical power, although each of them has many variations. Think of them as outer, inner, and all-around theories.

Outer theories about magic say that a magician's power comes from beings that exist outside the magician. Some people consider these outside beings to be demons—powerful forces that are evil, or at least unpredictable and dangerous. Other people think of the outside beings as forces for good and credit the magicians who work with them with tapping into divine knowledge.

Magic believed to involve the use of demons is sometimes called black magic, and it is generally considered evil, or harmful. The connection with

A grimoire from 1801 depicts a spirit named Cassiel, said to rule the planet Saturn.

demons gave magic its dark reputation and made it a crime or a sin in some societies. In Europe before the eighteenth century, for example, someone who studied magic risked being accused of witchcraft, which at that time was believed to come from Satan or his demonic servants.

The outside beings who are said to lend their power to magicians have also been called spirits, elementals, presences, or simply intelligences. They are not always clearly associated with good or evil, however. And some magical traditions say that the magician's task is to work with both good and evil, and to balance them.

According to the outer theories of magic, a magician operates by invoking the spirits or intelligences. This means calling them from the spiritual or invisible realm into the presence of the magician, and then telling them what to do. Even when the spirits are not demons, invocation is considered a very serious matter. Magicians often speak of powerful forces that can harm a magician who fails to take proper precautions. Such precautions often include some form of purification, perhaps by fasting, bathing, or wearing special clothing. Another precaution is the magic circle, which the magician creates on the floor. During a magical ceremony, the magician stays within this protective circle. If even a fingertip crosses the circle, the magician may find himself or herself at the mercy of strong, unruly magical energies (or the ritual simply won't work).

Some magicians, especially in modern times, have doubted that outside beings or intelligences exist. J. W. Brodie-Innes, for example, was a member of the Golden Dawn, a magical society founded in England in the 1880s. The Golden Dawn's teachings were said to have been passed down from ancient times by a band of hidden leaders called the Secret Chiefs. At Golden Dawn meetings, the supernatural intelligences summoned by the magicians were demons called "Qliphotic forces," a term from the Jewish mystical lore known as the Kabbalah. Yet Brodie-Innes himself

A nineteenth-century magician named Eliphas Levi wrote the instructions for this ceremony, which supposedly invokes a demon within a magic circle.

declared, "Whether the Gods, the Qliphotic forces or even the Secret Chiefs really exist is comparatively unimportant; the point is that the universe behaves as though they do." This view is echoed by people today who say, "I don't care how magic works—I just know that it does."

Some magical practitioners use meditation as a tool for focusing their thoughts.

Inner theories of magic appeal to many modern magicians. In this view of magic, the source of a magician's power does not lie in some outside realm. The power is inside the magician all the time. Instead of invoking a force or energy from outside, the magician evokes it, or draws it out from within. Preparations for evocation are usually activities to clear the mind, or to bring on a different state of consciousness, such as meditation, prayer, or self-hypnosis through music or dance. According to this view of magic, the spells and symbols that magicians use in rituals are not instructions to outside powers. They are tools for focusing and guiding the magician's own will. Magical writers sometimes call this kind of magic a journey of self-discovery, or the process of finding and expressing one's true self.

All-around theories of magic say that the source of a magician's power lies all around us in the universe. It is not located within the magician's mind, nor does it come from conscious beings, or intelligences, outside the magician. Instead, it is a force of nature that is not yet recognized. It seems supernatural to us only because we don't understand it. Modern magician Aleister Crowley seemed to share this view. He said, "The question of magick is a question of discovering and employing hitherto unknown forces of Nature."

People who take the all-around view of magic sometimes point out that electricity was once considered magical, before scientists began to understand its nature and properties. Gravity is another example—it influences everything in the universe, it links all objects through interconnected webs of force, yet it is completely invisible. Sir Isaac Newton, the English scientist who published his discovery of the law of universal gravitation in 1687, realized that saying that the earth and the moon acted on each other at a distance, through empty space, sounded like magic. He explained that gravitational relationships among objects were not "occult qualities" but "general laws of nature." The effects of gravity could be seen and studied, even though the cause of gravity remained hidden.

In 1972, Arthur C. Clarke, a British engineer and science fiction writer, said, "Any sufficiently advanced technology is indistinguishable from magic." Clarke meant that things that can't be explained look like magic. Ten thousand years ago, a simple match for lighting a fire would have seemed magical. Today it is a very basic piece of technology, and there is no mystery about the chemistry and physics that make it work. Could magic be the operation of natural forces not yet dreamed of by science? If so, then spells and rituals are the technology for harnessing these forces.

A client (*left*) consults a fortune-teller in early
twentieth-century France. The idea that cards and other objects
can be used to foretell the future is one of the oldest
and most widespread magical beliefs.

Stars, Spells, and the Philosopher's Stone

F rom alchemy to voodoo, there are hundreds of magical practices and traditions. They fall into three general categories, depending on what the magic is used for. The categories are divination, spells, and high magic. These three are not always separate—in fact, they often blend into one another, or intermingle. A grimoire might contain instructions for divination alongside a list of spells, for example, or a wizard might study high magic while using divination. Magic is always hard to pin down.

Divination

Divination is fortune-telling. More broadly, it is the use of magical or supernatural means to seek hidden knowledge. Divination is generally used by people who want to know the future, but it can also be concerned with matters in the present, such as the location of a lost treasure, or the most favorable date for a wedding. A magician might also turn to divination to learn someone else's secrets.

A fifteenth-century illustration shows medieval astrologers at work. Several of them have tools like those used for surveying and navigating, a reminder that many people of that time considered astrology a science.

Astrology is one of the best-known forms of divination. It has been practiced in many parts of the world for thousands of years, and it remains popular today. Other methods of divination have fallen out of style. The ancient art of haruspicy, or reading the future in the shape of a sacrificed animal's liver, is no longer widely used. Nor is scapulimancy, which means decoding the meaning of cracks in a burned bone—one of the first methods of divination known from ancient China.

Necromancy, calling up the spirits of the dead to communicate with them, was considered a dark and dangerous form of magic in the past, when sorcerers were thought to use it to gain forbidden knowledge. Today spirit communication is promoted by psychics and channelers who claim that they can put people in touch with their dead loved ones. They don't use the word *necromancy*, though—it doesn't fit the warm and comforting image of present-day "talking to the dead."

Some methods of divination use tools, such as tarot cards, tea leaves, Ouija boards, or the Chinese system called the I Ching, in which the diviner interprets the meaning of patterns spelled out by the tossing of coins or plant stalks. Bibliomancy is a form of divination in which a person seeking the answer to a question opens a book (often the Bible or another sacred book) at random and points to a place on the page. That passage of the text is interpreted as the answer.

Another kind of divination focuses on things that happen without any action on the diviner's part. Happenings that can be seen as signs of good or bad fortune are called omens. The ancient Romans had a very

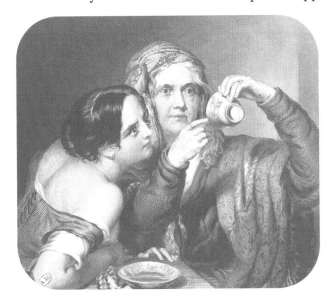

Is hidden knowledge revealed in ordinary tea leaves or coffee grounds? Some people today still think so.

highly developed system of omens. The position of a cloud, or the flight of a bird across the sky, was filled with meaning. Particularly bad omens, such as the births of deformed animals, were thought to foretell danger to the empire or its rulers. This belief was still strong in 814, when the emperor Charlemagne died. Dozens of omens, including an eclipse of the sun, were said to have occurred in the weeks leading up to his death.

Have you ever heard someone say, "That means seven years of bad luck" after breaking a mirror? Most people know of a few such superstitions, even if they don't take them seriously. Like spilling salt or walking under a ladder, a broken mirror is supposed to be a sign of what is to come—an omen.

Spells

When most people think of practicing magic, they think of spells. A spell is a magical act aimed at producing a specific result. A spell may have any or all of the following parts: a set of words to be recited, a formula for carrying out certain motions or actions, a potion or powder to be consumed, or a physical object such as a charm.

Spells are directed toward many kinds of goals. Curative spells are meant to heal someone, or, in a more public use, to rid a community of disease. Afflictive spells are intended to cause harm to someone. They may act directly on the target by bringing about injury, illness, misfortune, or death, or they may act indirectly by attacking the target's loved ones or possessions. (One of the most common accusations of witchcraft in earlier centuries was that the witch had used afflictive magic against the victim's livestock.)

Another kind of magic is the apotropaic spell, which is supposed to ward off harm. Apotropaic spells often take the form of protective charms called amulets. These might be symbols, pieces of text, bones or stones that have had magical words said over them, or gems believed to counteract certain kinds of threats, such as amethysts, which were once believed to guard their wearers against poison. In Italy and parts of eastern Europe and the Middle East, people wear amulets in the shape of a small hand with the index finger and little finger extended. This is a very old defense against the afflictive magic known as the "evil eye," a glance from a witch or magician that is thought to carry a curse.

A charm worn to attract good fortune is called a talisman. The material of a talisman can be exactly the same as the material of an apotropaic amulet—the dif-

Europe's magical tradition included the "wisewoman," who was often skilled in making herbal medicines.

ference is in the intention with which the magician creates the charm.

Spells can be enacted to bring good luck, money, pregnancy, or any other desired result. There is no single "recipe" for any of these outcomes. A medieval grimoire could offer many ways to achieve the same goal. Today, a typical well-stocked bookstore with

A woman pours a love potion into a drink. In some magical tales, the wrong person drinks a love potion, with results that range from comical to tragic.

a section on magic might have a dozen different books of love spells alone.

People have probably been using magic to win love for about as long as they have been using magic. Love spells have been found in magical writings from ancient India, Mesopotamia, Egypt, and other places. The Romans were big believers in love magic—even though many of their potions contained poisons or strong drugs that could have disastrous effects. The poet and philosopher Lucretius, according to some stories of his life, drank a love potion that drove him insane; under its influence, he committed suicide.

Love potions often included ingredients that had strong tastes, such as onions and pepper, or that gave a sensation of heat, such as ginger and cinnamon. Sometimes the ingredients were just plain disgusting, such as human remains. Often this took the form of powdered bone, but some recipes called for flesh. One love potion required the spleen and bone marrow of a young boy who had been murdered. Less horrible, but still unpleasant, was a traditional English love recipe: powdered periwinkle flowers and earthworms. It was supposed to be eaten with meat, perhaps to hide the taste.

The strongest kind of love charm had something from each of the two people it was supposed to affect. A magician could blend their hair, blood, possessions, or even words, such as their names, into charms. In some rituals, two people exchanged tokens, a magical act that was meant to bind them together (very similar to the marriage ceremony in which the couple exchange rings). In seventeenth-century England, lovers would break a silver coin in two, and each would keep a piece. The idea was that their love would last as long as each had the charm.

Magic could also be used to kill love. During the Middle Ages, for example, European magicians gave women "rings of oblivion [forgetting]" that caused them to forget about old loves. Another love-killing spell used an ointment made of mouse dung. (That one sounds quite effective!)

In spite of the great and lasting popularity of love magic, people generally considered it underhanded, or even criminal, to trick or force someone into falling in love by magical means. Whenever people disapproved of a match, rumors might hint that one of the parties had used magic to trap the other one. This was especially likely if the people in the match were royal or rich. After King Henry VIII of England divorced his first wife and married Anne Boleyn, accusations flew. Anne, it was said, had bewitched the king with illicit love spells! (She was also rumored to have six fingers on one hand—just the sort of "unnatural" feature that people saw as

Having an extra finger (count them) is called polydactyly. This condition is rare but natural, although it is sometimes linked to witchcraft.

the mark of a witch.) Nine years after their marriage, Parliament passed the Witchcraft Statute of 1542. Among other things, this law made it a felony to "practice or cause to be used . . . any invocation of spirites, witchcrafts, enchantments or sorcerers to . . . provoke any person to unlawful love."

High Magic

The magic of spells, curses, lucky charms, and fortune-telling has sometimes been called "low" magic. It is practical magic, meant to get immediate, definite results. A different kind of magic has a loftier, more philosophical goal: gaining knowledge or wisdom. The purpose of this "high" magic is to understand the universe, and therefore have power over it. High magic is sometimes called learned, theoretical, ritual, or ceremonial magic. Unlike low magic, which is based on traditional lore handed down from generation to generation among shamans or wisewomen in a community, high magic is based on the study of occult books. You might say it's magic for an elite, select few.

In Europe, high magic blossomed during the Renaissance. Starting around 1300, Europeans became fascinated with the knowledge and culture of the ancient world. While Europe was in the "dark" and Middle Ages, the Muslim world, which included southern Spain as well as the Middle East, had reached a high point in learning and civilization. Thanks to the efforts of Muslim scholars, many ancient Greek, Latin, and Hebrew writings were translated into Arabic and preserved for future generations. Muslim scholars contributed to the growth of science and medicine as well, producing their own learned texts. As contact between Europe and the Islamic world increased, Europeans began to discover more and more of the light of the ancient world. This process sped up after the eastern city of Constantinople fell to the Turks in 1453. Greek-speaking scholars fled Constantinople for western Europe, bringing with them still more ancient works on philosophy, religion—and magic. In particular, the writings of Hermes Trismegistus (the name means "Three Times Great Hermes") kicked off a boom in high magic in Italy and beyond.

Little was known about Hermes. He was believed to have lived in ancient Egypt at the time of Moses, and even to have met Moses. He was a man of great wisdom and learning, as well as a powerful magician. Some even identified him with the Egyptian god Thoth and the Greek god Hermes. The knowledge of Hermes Trismegistus was said to have traveled down the centuries in writings called the hermetic texts. When the scholars of the Renaissance got hold of these texts, they were astonished. All the brilliant ideas that they thought had come from famous Greek philosophers such as Plato were really Hermes' ideas—the Greeks had merely copied them. Hermes had even predicted the birth of Jesus. Surely he was the greatest magician of all time!

Fifteenth-century philosophers, artists, and religious scholars set about studying the hermetic writings with intense interest.

These works held out an incredible promise: Someone who succeeded in the difficult task of mastering the magical arts, someone who could understand the true inner meaning of their symbols and rituals, would be more than a magician. That

People of the Renaissance honored Hermes Trismegistus as the wisest magician of the ancient world.

person would be like a god, with ultimate knowledge of the true workings of the universe—and ultimate power.

Alchemy was one branch of magic that flourished during the Renaissance under the influence of hermeticism, although it had existed much earlier. Today alchemy is often seen as an early form of such sciences as chemistry and metallurgy. Alchemists were concerned with the properties of the physical world. Like modern scientists, they worked in laboratories and performed experiments.

Renaissance alchemists made many breakthroughs. They designed laboratory equipment and procedures, manufactured dyes and chemical extracts, worked with explosives, and found new ways of making glass and refining metals. Today we would call these things scientific, or technological. For alchemists, though, their meaning went beyond the physical world. Elements and processes were symbols with magical or spiritual meaning, just like the words and signs used in spells. For example, some alchemists thought that mercury, sulfur, and salt corresponded to water, fire, and earth, and also to the spirit, soul, and body. By properly manipulating and combining these ingredients, or others such as lead, the alchemist hoped to produce the highest state of all: gold, which corresponded to air and to immortality.

But the alchemists were not simply trying to turn worthless lead into precious gold. Their quest was even more ambitious than that. They believed that the process of turning "low" materials into gold, called transmutation, would bring a corresponding change to the magician, who would be transmuted into a higher being.

The alchemists' most sought-after goal was the philosopher's stone—although it wasn't necessarily a stone. Various alchemists described it as a gem, a powder, or a liquid. Whatever its form, it was the most precious thing in existence, filled with a divine power. Anything touched by the philosopher's stone would be healed, purified, transmuted, and perfected. A magician who possessed it would remain youthful and healthy forever.

You couldn't just find the philosopher's stone, though. You had to make it by refining and purifying common, low elements into higher and higher ones. The problem was that no one knew exactly how this process was supposed to work, or what elements to start with.

In their quest for the philosopher's stone, alchemists developed hundreds of theories and carried out thousands of experiments. Many figures whom we now think of as scientists, such as Sir Isaac Newton, took alchemy seriously and devoted much time and effort to it. Once in a while an alchemist claimed to have found the philosopher's stone, or the elixir of life, a potion that was supposed to grant immortality. In the eighteenth century, a magician named the Count of St. Germain made such a claim. He had, he declared, lived for two thousand years. Occasionally he would mention conversations he had had in the distant past with such famous figures as Cleopatra or Jesus. But in 1784 St. Germain died, proving that he was as mortal as the rest of us.

In their desperate and unsuccessful search for the philosopher's stone, alchemists sometimes turned to fraud. In 1782, a young Englishman named James Price announced that he had produced the stone. He gave demonstrations in which a red powder appeared to turn mercury into gold. From today's point of view, it seems clear that he was using stage magic to pull off the

Seventeenth-century Flemish painter David Teniers filled *The Alchemist* with the equipment these early chemists used in their quest for the deepest secrets of the universe.

trick. Some leading scientific thinkers of his time seem to have thought so, too. They went to Price's laboratory so that he could perform his ritual in front of them, but his nerve failed him. As the horrified scientists looked on, Price drank a flask of acid and died before their eyes.

By that time, the modern sciences of chemistry and physics were taking shape. Because science was interested in discovering testable, provable things about the world—things that were

Roger Bacon, a thirteenth-century English church-man and scholar, was interested in hermetic lore as well as in the sciences.

consistently true, not dependent upon a magician's inner strength or control of spirits—it turned away from the magical, philosophical, spiritual quest of the alchemists. Another blow to alchemy came from literary scholars and historians who examined the hermetic texts with a critical eye. Their findings killed Hermes Trismegistus, the great magician of the ancient world.

The hermetic texts, it turned out, had been written by many different people, not by a single sage. And they were not nearly as old as the Renaissance scholars and magicians thought. They dated from three to five centuries after the time of Christ (and even longer after the time of Plato and the other Greek philosophers).

Much of the material in the hermetic texts came from sources such as ancient Middle Eastern and Greek mythology, early Christian texts, and traditional Jewish mystical writings. The unknown hermetic authors had mixed these and other ingredients into what one modern history of magical practices calls a "wild brew of Greek philosophy, alchemy, and magic." But even though Hermes Trismegistus never existed, the symbols, rituals, and theories of high magic inspired some of history's best-known magicians, wizards, and sorcerers.

Solar eclipses were once thought to be omens of dire calamities.
They occur when the moon passes between the earth and
the sun, blotting out the sun and darkening the day.

Wizards and Sorcerers

Magic was in the air in Rome during the summer of 1630. The whole city was buzzing with rumors about frightening predictions and forbidden rituals. Wherever people gathered to gossip, they spread the news: The city's most famous astrologer had declared that Pope Urban VIII would soon die! An eclipse of the sun was coming, and the astrologer knew from the pope's horoscope that the eclipse would be fatal to him.

Word of the inauspicious horoscope spread quickly. Letters carried the news through Italy, then on to France and Spain. Ambitious church leaders started looking ahead, wondering who the next pope would be. But the most shocking part of the story wasn't the prediction. It was the rumor that the pope himself had already taken part in an illegal magical rite. The scandal would end in a trial, the suspicious death of an astrologer, and a stern new law against magic.

One Magician's Fate

The rumors about Pope Urban VIII actually started in 1629, when a scholar named Tommaso Campanella published *De siderali*

Pope Urban VIII feared eclipses—but would he turn to magic to protect himself from them?

fato vitando (*How to Avoid the Fate Dictated by the Stars*). Campanella was an astrologer, and like all astrologers, he believed that the movements of the heavenly bodies corresponded to events in the lives of people on Earth. Comets and eclipses were especially feared. They were warnings of war, destruction, or the deaths of powerful people—and no one in Rome was more powerful than the pope, who was both the head of the Roman Catholic Church and the monarch of central Italy.

But Campanella also believed that people could change the effects of the heavenly bodies. If your horoscope said that you were going to die during the next eclipse, for example, you could "cancel out" the eclipse by performing certain magical actions. Campanella told how this could be done, and he was speaking from experience. Just a year earlier, in 1628, he had performed a magical ritual to save the pope.

At that time, Urban VIII had feared the deadly effects of an eclipse of the moon. Urban took astrology seriously—so seriously that he regularly ordered astrologers to cast horoscopes for high-ranking church officials so that he would know when they were supposed to die. When his own horoscope showed danger from the lunar eclipse of 1628, Urban asked Campanella to do something about it.

Campanella picked out a room in the Lateran Palace, where the pope lived, and had its walls covered with white silk. Inside the room he positioned two lamps to represent the sun and moon. He added five torches for the five planets that were known at the time: Mercury, Venus, Mars, Jupiter, and Saturn. Because Jupiter, Venus, and the sun were helpful forces in the horoscope, able to fight the eclipse's harmful effects, Campanella placed in the room a selection of gems, plants, and perfumes believed to be linked to those three heavenly bodies. He also recommended that at the time of the eclipse certain music, which would attract the favorable influences of Jupiter and Venus, be played.

Campanella was working according to the magical principle of "As below, so above." By creating a harmless arrangement of the heavenly bodies here below, he would cancel out the dangerous eclipse of the moon above. The pope waited out the eclipse in this protective chamber, with the doors and windows sealed to prevent any "seeds" of the eclipse from drifting in on the air. There he sat, listening to the proper music and burning rosemary and other scented plants.

The ritual didn't stop the eclipse of the moon from happening, but it did appear to protect Urban VIII, for the pope managed to survive the dreaded event. And Campanella must have thought that his magic had worked, for the next year he described the entire ceremony in his astrological book.

That book was a problem for Urban VIII. The pope didn't want it to be known that he had taken part in magical practices, because the church frowned on such things. In fact, the pope before Urban, Gregory XV, had issued a strong statement against magicians and witches. Although many educated people of the time studied astrology and other aspects of magic in the same way that they studied religion and the beginnings of science, the church officially condemned all things magical and disapproved of divination, including astrology. So gossip about the ritual at the Lateran Palace would not be good for the pope.

Campanella tried to patch things up by rushing another work into print. It was called *Apologeticus*. In it Campanella tried to defend his actions by saying that his directions for "avoiding the fate dictated by the stars" weren't magical or superstitious. By that time, though, Urban VIII had another problem, this one connected with the eclipse of the sun. Orazio Morandi, a well-known astrologer in Rome, had predicted that the coming solar eclipse would bring death to the pope.

The pope found himself in a difficult position. If he sought magical protection from the eclipse, he would only create more damaging rumors. So he decided to come down on the side of the church's official position, taking action against magic. He had Morandi arrested and thrown into jail.

Up to that point, Morandi had succeeded in the balancing act that magicians had to perform in Christian Europe before modern times. Students of magic who had powerful friends, who were careful not to call too much attention to themselves, or who tried not to offend the church were usually regarded as philosophers. Morandi, for example, was a friend of many well-known artists, scholars, and even cardinals, who are high officials in the church. He gave the cardinals advice on occult matters, and in return they protected him.

But if astrologers or magicians offended people in power, created trouble, or promoted ideas that went too strongly against church teachings, they could be tried for religious crimes. Even though Pope Urban VIII and many other church leaders believed in astrology, the church officially condemned it, claiming that divination was an attempt to seize knowledge that belongs only to God. Astrology was also related to other forbidden magical practices, such as witchcraft,

An astrologer in Renaissance Europe could be respected as a scholar or condemned as a sorcerer.

that the Bible called evil. So Morandi found himself in a cell in Rome's Tor di Nona prison.

On November 7, 1630, Morandi died in that cell. The official cause of death was fever. The gossips of Rome, though, had other ideas. A historian named Giacinto Gigli wrote, "It is believed without a doubt that [Morandi] was killed by poison administered through his food." Who was responsible for this supposed poisoning? Many suspected the pope, who wanted to silence Morandi's talk of eclipses and papal death.

As Morandi's fate shows, being a magician can be risky. Over the centuries, magical practitioners have held all kinds of positions in society. Some have been honored and influential. Others have been feared, persecuted, or neglected. Even the names applied to magicians have had various meanings. Anyone who practiced the occult arts could be called a magician. Such people might also be called witches, especially if they practiced low rather than high magic. To make things even more confusing, *wizard* was sometimes another name for a male witch and sometimes a term for a high magician. The label *sorcerer* often held shades of dark, dangerous meaning. It was used for those who dealt with powerful, possibly demonic forces, or who were believed to work destructive magic. Most feared of all was the necromancer, a magician who was thought to raise the spirits of the dead.

Famous Wizards and Sorcerers

Early wizards and sorcerers live in the shadowy borderland between reality and imagination. Some of them were real historical figures, although tales about their magical deeds are legends. A few may be purely fictional. Historians can't untangle the stories told about them from any threads of fact they may contain.

Pythagoras of Samos, a Greek mathematician and philosopher of the sixth century B.C.E.,* has been called a magician, although it's impossible to separate Pythagoras's own beliefs and teachings

---

*A variety of systems of dating have been used by different cultures throughout history. Many historians now prefer to use B.C.E. (Before Common Era) and C.E. (Common Era) instead of B.C. (Before Christ) and A.D. (Anno Domini), out of respect for the diversity of the world's peoples.

Raphael, an Italian artist of the sixteenth century, depicted the ancient mathematician Pythagoras as a wise old man passing his mystical knowledge on to the young.

from the ideas that his students and followers developed. The Pythagoreans, as they are called, believed that mathematics was the key to understanding the true nature of the universe. Many modern mathematicians might agree, but Pythagoras and his followers also practiced rituals—including following a vegetarian diet, keeping silent, and listening to music and poetry—that were meant to reveal hidden wisdom to them. Among other things, the Pythagoreans believed that souls could leave their bodies to travel through time and space.

Apollonius of Tyana was another ancient Greek with a reputation for wizardry. Born in the city of Tyana in what is now Turkey,

Apollonius of Tyana, who lived at about the time of Christ, was said to have had many powers, including raising the dead.

Apollonius lived during the first century C.E. and was much influenced by Pythagorean ideas. He was said to have spent seven years in complete silence, and then to have traveled through Persia and India to study the wisdom of magicians and sages in those lands. Later stories about Apollonius said that he had wondrous powers: seeing the future, speaking to the dead, and bringing the dead back to life. In 272, two centuries after Apollonius's time, the Roman emperor Aurelian was ready to attack Tyana when, the emperor reported, Apollonius appeared to him in a dream or vision and urged him to spare the city. (He did.)

Merlin, the powerful wizard who was the guide and adviser to Britain's King Arthur, is one of the most famous magicians of all. Like Arthur himself, Merlin has been the subject of both historical research and wild guesswork. How "real" these characters were is a matter of debate. Arthur and Merlin first became widely known from the writings of a twelfth-century British historian named Geoffrey of Monmouth. He may have based them—loosely—on some historical figures, but the stories that formed around them are legends, filled with things borrowed from the folklore, poetry, and literature of the Middle Ages.

Many marvels were credited to Merlin. Some said that he built Stonehenge, a great circle of huge standing stones in the English countryside, by using magic to move the stones. Merlin employed his powers of enchantment to make a king named Uther Pendragon look like another man, so that Uther could father a child with that man's wife. As a wizard, Merlin possessed the power of prophecy, and he knew that the son born of their union would become King Arthur.

Merlin, it was said, foretold the entire future of Britain. He even foresaw his own doom, which came about through a combination of love and sorcery. Merlin fell in love with a young women named Nimue.

But after Nimue coaxed Merlin into teaching her the secrets of his magic, she used the knowledge to cast him under a spell of imprisonment. Some stories about Merlin say that he still sleeps hidden in some unknown place, and that he and King Arthur will return one day, when Britain desperately needs them.

According to legend, the magician Merlin was the teacher and adviser of Britain's King Arthur. The character Merlin may have come from Welsh mythology.

Magic, science, and religion mingled harmoniously in the career of a thirteenth-century German scholar known as Albertus Magnus, or Albert the Great. He became a member of the Dominican religious order, and later a bishop in the Roman Catholic Church. Albertus devoted much time to studying philosophy and the natural world. He also practiced alchemy—one of his achievements was identifying the element arsenic. Albertus's wide learning, along with his interest in subjects bordering on the occult, led some envious and hostile people to accuse him of being a magician. It was even said that he had had dealings with the devil. These accusations did no lasting harm to Albertus, who was made a saint of the Roman Catholic Church in 1931. He is considered the patron saint of scientists and philosophers.

Albertus was rumored to have built a magical metal head that could answer any question. The idea of a magical talking head must have fascinated people in the Middle Ages, because the same feat was credited to another thirteenth-century

In the thirteenth century, too much knowledge could be dangerous. But Albertus Magnus survived accusations of sorcery to become a saint.

philosopher-scientist, Roger Bacon of England. Sadly, no evidence of such a head has ever been found. Bacon, who promoted the idea that well-designed experiments were a good way to investigate the natural world, practiced both astrology and alchemy. He also knew a number of languages. This has led some researchers of magic to suggest that Bacon was the author of a mysterious work called the Voynich manuscript.

The Voynich manuscript is a handwritten, illustrated book of more than two hundred pages.

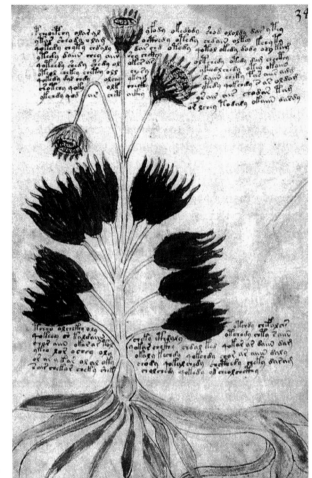

A book of secret knowledge—or a hoax? No one knows, because no one has been able to decode the mysterious Voynich manuscript.

It was once the property of a seventeenth-century Polish alchemist, but its history is confused, to say the least. The manuscript came to light in 1912 when a book dealer named Voynich got hold of it. Today it is held at Yale University in Connecticut. Experts in the dating of old documents think that it was written around 1500, which was after Bacon's time.

The characters in which the manuscript is written don't match any known script, and the words they seem to form have no recognizable link to any known language. Perhaps the manuscript is in code—but hundreds of highly skilled code breakers, among them military analysts and computer geniuses, have tried to crack it. None has succeeded. Some experts think that the whole thing is a meaningless jumble, perhaps a hoax. Yet others suspect that the Voynich manuscript, which contains many drawings of plants next to lists that look like recipes, is a treasure-house of hidden knowledge about herbal medicine, magical spells, or both.

John Dee has also been suggested as the possible author of the puzzling manuscript. Dee was an English mathematician, scientist, and occultist who lived in sixteenth-century England. He served as astrological adviser to Queen Elizabeth I and wrote about magic. Later he turned to spirit communication and magical rites. He produced several works on occult subjects that, he said, were dictated to him by angels. Dee fell on hard times in his later years. For a time he held a job at a church in Manchester, given to him by Queen Elizabeth. But King James I, who followed Elizabeth on the throne, was hostile to the supernatural and occult, and John Dee died in poverty and neglect.

One of the most famous and far-traveling magicians of the Renaissance was a physician named Philippus Aureolus Theophrastus Bombast von Hohenheim. Later in life he adopted the simpler name Paracelsus. He was drawn to alchemy not because he hoped to turn lead into gold, but because he believed that alchemy might hold the keys to healing. He was especially interested in understanding how medicines worked, and in finding better ones.

Paracelsus traveled for much of his life, practicing medicine and studying under local doctors in Egypt, the Near East, Arabia,

Occultist and mathematician John Dee is said to have used astrology to choose the date of Queen Elizabeth's coronation in 1558.

and many parts of eastern and central Europe. For Paracelsus, the healing arts and the magical arts were intertwined. He possessed a great deal of practical medical knowledge—the kind of knowledge that today would be called scientific—but he also used astrology and talismans to treat his patients. "Magic has power to experience and fathom things which are inaccessible to human reason," Paracelsus wrote. "For magic is a great secret wisdom, just as reason is a great public folly."

During the nineteenth century, magic lost some of its secrecy, largely through the work of Abbé Louis Constant, a Frenchman who took the magical name Eliphas Levi. Starting in 1856, he published a series of books on occultism, including *Transcendental Magic, The History of Magic,* and *The Key of the Mysteries.* According to Levi, adepts—people who penetrated the mysteries of the occult and practiced magic—should follow four rules: to know, to dare, to will, and to keep silent. Yet Richard Cavendish, a modern historian of magic, has pointed out that "this instruction to keep silent occurs in one of the longest and most revealing books about magic ever written."

Paracelsus, a Swiss-born physician of the early sixteenth century, treated his patients with a combination of medicine and magic.

Levi's most famous magical feat was said to be conjuring up the spirit of the ancient sorcerer Apollonius of Tyana. It happened while he was in England, visiting the writer Edward Bulwer-Lytton, who was extremely interested in occult matters. Levi already had a reputation as a learned magician, and he found that people expected him to perform miracles and give demonstrations of his occult skills. He had always avoided such things, but while staying with Bulwer-Lytton he agreed to perform a ritual, although he insisted that no one else be present at the time. In a building on Bulwer-Lytton's estate that had been specially prepared for the occasion, Levi summoned Apollonius. According to Levi, the ritual worked, and the spirit of Apollonius appeared. Levi also said, however, that he believed the experience happened only in his own mind. Soon afterward he returned to Paris, where he spent the rest of his life writing and teaching the secrets of the Kabbalah and the tarot cards to pupils.

Helena Petrovna Blavatsky, who preferred to be called HPB, was another nineteenth-century magician. She was more famous than Levi, but not all of the fame was good. Blavatsky was accused of fraud, fakery, and fabrication, yet she also built up a reputation for amazing psychic and magical feats and founded an influential occult group.

Born in Ukraine, Blavatsky claimed to have run away at eighteen from an unhappy marriage, and then to have spent years traveling all over the world. Her experiences during this time were varied: among other things, she claimed to have worked as a bareback rider in a circus in Istanbul, Turkey, and to have lived for two years in Tibet, studying the occult. (Some of her critics later scoffed that if Blavatsky had done only half the things she claimed to have done, she would have had a remarkable life.) Throughout her life Blavatsky said she was guided by spiritual beings she had met in Tibet. Called the Masters, or Mahatmas, they had chosen her to reveal their hidden truths to the world.

In 1874 Blavatsky went to New York City, where she impressed many people with her powers. Two of her specialties were communicating with the dead and materializing objects out of thin air.

HPB, as Helena Petrovna Blavatsky liked to be called, was one of the most noted—or notorious—occultists of the nineteenth century.

The next year she founded an occult organization called the Theosophical Society, and two years after that she published *Isis Unveiled*, the first of her works on occult subjects. Blavatsky claimed that all religions, and all forms of magic, were the scattered fragments of an ancient body of knowledge that she called the "secret doctrine," a source of great power and wisdom.

Blavatsky moved the headquarters of the Theosophical Society to India in 1879. Soon visitors to her home were reporting a steady stream of miraculous, magical occurrences: letters from the Masters fell into HPB's hands out of thin air, bells rang in empty rooms, and the spirit of one of the Masters could be seen in the garden at night. Stories about these events aroused new interest in HPB. Riding a wave of publicity, she went to England in 1884, and the Society for Psychical Research (SPR), a British organization devoted to the scientific study of the supernatural, asked to test her powers.

Just then, awkward news arrived from India. Assistants who had been left in charge of HPB's house there confessed that they had helped her perform her "miracles." They claimed that there was a special suit made to look like a ghost, and that the mysterious letters were really passed through concealed slots in the walls and ceilings. The truth of these and other accusations against HPB is still hotly debated by critics and believers, although the SPR made its opinion perfectly clear when it said, "For our own part, we regard [Blavatsky] neither as the mouthpiece of hidden seers, nor as a mere vulgar adventuress; we think that she has achieved a title to permanent remembrance as one of the most accomplished, ingenious, and interesting imposters in history."

Blavatsky's main contribution to magic did not lie in the feats she may or may not have performed, or even in the secret doctrine she tried to reveal to the world. Her main contribution was in reawakening an interest in the occult. Blavatsky helped pave the way for what some have called New Age magic, a popular blend of European and Asian mystical traditions.

Today, in the early years of the twenty-first century, interest in magic shows no sign of disappearing. In fact, according to journalist Christine Wicker, "[S]ome people believe a great magical renaissance is beginning." As old as the first hunting dance, as new as the latest Internet site about the Kabbalah, magic has not yet lost its power over our imaginations.

LA DOMENICA DEL CORRIERE

Anno L. 10.— ESTERO L. 20.—
Semestre " 5,50 " 11,—

Per le inserzioni rivolgersi all'Amministrazione del Corriere della Sera - Via Solferino, 28 - Milano.

Si pubblica a Milano ogni settimana

Supplemento illustrato del " Corriere della Sera ,,

Uffici del giornale:
Via Solferino, 28, Milano

Per tutti gli articoli e illustrazioni è riservata la proprietà letteraria e artistica, secondo le leggi e i trattati internazionali.

Anno XXVI — Num 8.   24 Febbraio 1924.   Centesimi 20 la copia.

La luce finalmente nelle tenebre trimillenarie di Tutankamen.
La scena culminante degli scavi di Luxor: il primo sguardo nel sontuoso sarcofago del re egizio.

(Disegno di A. Beltrame)

Howard Carter opens the shrine holding Tutankhamen's sarcophagus, or stone coffin. Did Carter's entry into the pharaoh's tomb trigger an ancient curse?

What Do You Think?

Lord Carnarvon died in an Egyptian hospital just a few weeks after the official opening of King Tutankhamen's burial chamber. His illness stemmed from an infected mosquito bite. Could it have been the death that was supposed to come "on wings" to those who dared violate a pharaoh's tomb?

Certainly many newspaper writers thought so—or at least they realized that a mummy's curse could sell a lot of newspapers. And Carnarvon's death was only the first. Three years later, a French Egyptologist named Georges Bénédite, who had witnessed the tomb opening, died of heatstroke. Two years after that, Arthur C. Mace of New York's Metropolitan Museum also died. Newspapers announced these deaths with headlines like "Mummy's Curse Strikes Again!"

The public became firmly convinced that people connected with the excavation of King Tut's tomb, or with the examination of his mummy, were dying at an unnatural rate. Some people thought the deaths were being caused by magical spells. Others suggested that the tomb had been booby-trapped with tiny poisonous darts, or that a disease germ had survived in the burial chamber for three thousand years to infect those who entered it.

Carnarvon was the first person associated with the opening of Tut's tomb to die—but not the last.

The idea of a mummy's curse on tomb robbers made a lot of people decide to get rid of souvenirs they had once treasured. Museums received surprising donations of things that tourists had picked up during their travels in Egypt. Someone even sent the British Museum a mummy's arm. Egyptologists also received a steady stream of letters from people asking about the curse.

In 1934 Herbert E. Winlock of the Metropolitan Museum made a list of the twenty-six people who had been present when the burial chamber was opened. He then checked to see how many of them had died within ten years of the opening. The number of deaths, Winlock discovered, was six. Of the people who had been present when King Tutankhamen's mummy was unwrapped, none had died. Some of the deaths that had occurred could easily be explained without any mention of a curse. Bénédite was sixty-nine years old. Mace had been seriously ill with pleurisy long before the tomb was opened. And Carnarvon was known to have been in poor health for many years before coming to the Valley of the Kings.

Winlock kept a list called "Victims of the Curse, According to the Newspaper Reporters." On the list he noted falsehoods and mistakes in articles about King Tut's curse. One article, for example, reported that a worker in the British Museum had dropped dead while labeling items from the tomb. Winlock wrote, "But there are no objects from the tomb in the British Museum and never have been." Another supposed "victim" was an Egyptian prince, murdered in a London hotel by his French wife. He had no connection with the archaeological dig, and there was no evidence that he had ever been near the tomb. For years Winlock sent corrections to the newspapers, but the story of the mummy's curse lived on.

More recently, James Randi, a professional illusionist who has taken a leading role in debunking supernatural and occult claims, put together his own list of deaths connected with the tomb of Tut. Randi located as many of the death reports as he could find. He discovered that the average life span of those connected with the opening of Tut's tomb was

If anyone should have been punished for violating the tomb, it was Carter, shown here opening the coffin. Yet he lived for years afterward.

actually one year longer than was typical for people of their time and social class.

Two people who *should* have been killed by the curse didn't die until years later. Carter, the tomb's discoverer, died sixteen years afterward, at the age of sixty-six. Lord Carnarvon's daughter Evelyn Herbert lived until 1980. Those two shared with Lord Carnarvon a secret that didn't come out until many years after the opening of the tomb. On the night of the discovery, Carter, Carnarvon, and Herbert did more than explore the outer rooms of the tomb. They entered the inner chamber to look around. Afterward, they covered up the evidence, making it look as though no one had gone into the inner chamber before the official ceremony. So those three were the original violators of the tomb. If a curse existed, it missed two-thirds of them.

The notion that King Tutankhamen's treasure carried a curse has lingered for decades, despite a lack of evidence.

The idea of a mummy's curse didn't start with the discovery of King Tut's tomb. It was a very old idea that had appeared in popular fiction. In the 1820s a young Englishwoman named Jane Webb published a novel called *The Mummy.* Set in the twenty-second century, it featured a mummy seeking revenge on a scholar. The American writer Louisa May Alcott, better known as the author of *Little Women,* wrote a story called "Lost in a Pyramid; or, The Mummy's Curse" that was published in a magazine in 1869. Other writers also used the idea. As a result, when Carter and Carnarvon opened King Tutankhamen's tomb in 1923, and then Carnarvon got sick, the idea of a mummy's curse popped at once into many people's minds.

As soon as Carnarvon died, people began adding to the story and twisting it to make it scarier or more exciting. Take the business about the lights going out in Cairo at the moment of Carnarvon's death. It didn't happen. The lights *did* go out in the hospital at around the time he died, though. To someone who thought Carnarvon had been slain by the curse of a long-dead mummy, sudden darkness in the hospital might be just as spooky as darkness over the whole city. Yet accounts of life in Cairo in the 1920s show that electrical blackouts in buildings or neighborhoods were extremely common. There is no way to prove that the loss of light in Carnarvon's hospital had any special meaning—and no way to prove that it didn't. Just as there's no way to know whether Carnarvon's dog really howled at the moment of his death, or what that might mean if it were true.

Even before King Tut's tomb was found, mummies fascinated people. They had even appeared in movies. Most of the early films were short, forgettable comedies, such as *The Mummy and the Cow-puncher* (1912) and *Oh! You Mummy* (1914). The excitement over the curse of King Tut inspired a horror movie called *The Mummy* (1932), starring Boris Karloff. It told of the terrible fate that fell upon archaeologists who defied a curse and opened a mummy's tomb—a story that was destined to be repeated in many, many later films.

Like the newspapers of Carter's day, moviemakers found the "mummy's curse" to be irresistible. Films played with the idea that the ancient Egyptians had harnessed magical forces.

Today, even people who don't believe in the magical power of curses are convinced that the ancient Egyptians routinely placed curses on their tombs to protect the mummies and their treasures from tomb robbers. Television and movies feed this idea. Archaeology tells us that the truth was somewhat different.

No written curse was found in Tutankhamen's tomb or on his grave goods. Such curses were not particularly common, although archaeologists have found warnings in some Egyptian tombs. Often a stone tablet was placed at the entrance to a tomb, telling people to find their own burial place and not try to crowd into a tomb that already had someone in it. (This happened a lot in old Egypt. People with a dead relative to entomb would simply take over an existing burial site.) Other inscriptions were curses against anyone who harmed the tomb. Most of these curses were aimed at people who stole money from the "bank accounts" that were set up at temples to pay for guards for the tombs, but some were directed at robbers. A typical curse from around five thousand years ago reads, "As for any people who shall take possession of this tomb as their mortuary property, or shall do any evil thing to it, judgment shall be had by them for it with the great God."

Mysteries remain about the ancient Egyptians and their beliefs. We may never know exactly how they built the pyramids, or why their gods were portrayed with animal heads. But we do know that the ancient Egyptians, like many people throughout history, believed in spells and curses, in amulets and divination and the power of magicians to hurt or help people. In short, they believed in magic. Do you?

Glossary

alchemy An early form of experimental chemistry that later developed mystical, supernatural, and superstitious elements related to magic.

astrology A form of divination based on the belief that the positions and movements of the planets affect human life; the practice of foretelling someone's future using those movements.

debunking Proving that a supernatural or paranormal claim is false, or at least suspicious, by providing a natural explanation, pointing out holes or weaknesses in the claim, or exposing a hoax.

divination Originally, finding the will of the gods; now used more generally to mean fortune-telling, or seeing the future.

Kabbalah A body of Jewish mystical traditions spanning nearly two thousand years, from the first through the eighteenth centuries C.E. Elements of Kabbalah can be found in certain Jewish sects today.

magic The supposed power of individuals to control events in the world through secret knowledge or supernatural powers; sometimes called "magick" to set it apart from stage magic, or performing illusions for entertainment; may be divided into good (white) magic or harmful (black) magic.

necromancy Communication with the spirits of the dead for purposes of gaining knowledge; sometimes linked to sinful or forbidden knowledge, or practices such as sorcery or black magic.

occult Hidden, secret, as in hidden knowledge and secret practices; usually refers to the supernatural or magical.

prophecy Foretelling the future, often linked to religious belief or ceremony.

psychic One who claims paranormal or supernatural powers, such as seeing the future, reading minds, or communicating with the dead.

skeptic One who requires extraordinary proof of extraordinary claims and uses critical thinking to test statements.

sorcerer Magician, especially one thought to practice harmful or dangerous magic.

sorcery Magical practices; often has a negative meaning, as in black magic.

witch One who practices witchcraft.

witchcraft Method or art of using magical, supernatural, or mystical powers to influence events and people.

wizard Male witch or magician, although the term *witch* can be used for men as well as women.

For Further Research

Books

Alexander, Dominic. *Spellbound: From Ancient Gods to Modern Merlins, a Time Tour of Myth and Magic*. Pleasantville, NY: Reader's Digest, 2002.

Hill, Douglas. *Witches and Magic-Makers*. 2nd ed. New York: Dorling Kindersley, 2000.

Ogden, Tom. *Wizards and Sorcerers: From Abracadabra to Zoroaster*. New York: Facts On File, 1997.

Roleff, Tamara L., ed. *Black Magic and Witches*. San Diego, CA: Greenhaven, 2003.

Time-Life Books. *Magical Arts*. Alexandria, VA: Time-Life Books, 1990.

Waters, Fiona. *Wizard Tales: Stories of Enchantment and Magic from Around the World*. London: Pavilion, 2002.

Web Sites

www.llewellynencyclopedia.com/subjects.php?gen_sub=Magic+and+Ritual
   An online encyclopedia with brief articles or definitions for many topics connected with magic and occultism.

www.bbc.co.uk/history/ancient/egyptians/magic_01.shtml
   These easy-to-read "Ancient Egyptian Magic" pages give an overview of magical beliefs and practices among the ancient Egyptians, from scorpion charming to guarding the wisdom of the gods.

www.skepdic.com/magick.html
   * *The Skeptic's Dictionary* is an Internet reference that covers supernatural and paranormal topics "from abracadabra to zombies." Its "Magick" page briefly defines supernatural magic and has links to additional resources, while its page on "Magical Thinking" explores the psychology of magic. *The Skeptic's Dictionary* also offers a set of mini lessons in critical thinking.

www.lib.umich.edu/pap/magic/intro.html
   A University of Michigan collection of information and images related to magical beliefs and practices in the ancient world.

www.levity.com/alchemy/home.html
   The Alchemy Web Site has links to articles about alchemy, illustrations of alchemists and their activities, and more.

---

* Web site that will help develop critical thinking

Selected Bibliography

The author found these resources especially helpful when researching and writing this book.

Burton, Dan, and David Grandy. *Magic, Mystery, and Science: The Occult in Western Civilization*. Bloomington: Indiana University Press, 2004.

Butler, Elizabeth M. *Ritual Magic*. University Park: Pennsylvania State University Press, 1999.

Cavendish, Richard, ed. *Man, Myth, & Magic: The Illustrated Encyclopedia of Mythology, Religion, and the Unknown*. 21 vols. New York: Marshall Cavendish, 1995.

Drury, Nevill. *Magic and Witchcraft: From Shamanism to the Technopagans*. New York: Thames and Hudson, 2003.

Godwin, William. *Lives of the Necromancers*. 1876. Reprint, New York: Gordon, 1976.

Peters, Edward. *The Magician, the Witch, and the Law*. Philadelphia: University of Pennsylvania Press, 1978.

Ryan, W. F. *The Bathhouse at Midnight: Magic in Russia*. University Park: Pennsylvania State University Press, 1999.

Seligmann, Kurt. *A History of Magic and the Occult*. New York: Gramercy, 1997.

Wicker, Christine. *Not in Kansas Anymore: A Curious Tale of How Magic Is Transforming America*. New York: HarperSanFrancisco, 2005.

Notes

Is It True?

Tutankhamen curse from *Egypt: Land of the Pharaohs*, Alexandria, VA: Time-Life Books, 1992, pp. 119–134 and Dan Burton and David Grandy, *Magic, Mystery, and Science: The Occult in Western Civilization*, Bloomington: Indiana University Press, 2004, pp. 31–33 and "Curse of King Tut's Tomb," online at www.mummytombs.com/egypt/kingtut.html; David Keys, "Curse of the Mummy Invented by Victorian Writers," online at www.egyptvoyager.com/articles_curseofmummy.html and James Randi, "Tut, curse of king," in *Encyclopedia of Claims, Frauds, and Hoaxes of the Occult and Supernatural*, online at www. randi.org/encyclopedia/Tut,%20Curse%20of%20King.html

Napkin anecdote cited in Burton and Grandy, p. 39.

Proof quote from Christine Wicker, *Not in Kansas Anymore: A Curious Tale of How Magic Is Transforming America*, New York: HarperSanFrancisco, 2005, p. 66.

Chapter 1: Ancient Mysteries

Hoqarnaq ritual from Knud Rasmussen, *Thulefahrt* (1925), cited in Andreas Lommel, *Shamanism: The Beginnings of Art*, New York: McGraw-Hill, 1967, pp. 79–83.

"Third current" from Dan Burton and David Grandy, *Magic, Mystery, and Science: The Occult in Western Civilization*, Bloomington: Indiana University Press, 2004, p. 2.

Chapter 2: The Power of Magic

Russian grain doll from W. F. Ryan, *The Bathhouse at Midnight: Magic in Russia*, University Park: Pennsylvania State University Press, 1999, p. 36.

Crowley's fears from Dan Burton and David Grandy, *Magic, Mystery, and Science: The Occult in Western Civilization*, Bloomington: Indiana University Press, 2004, p. 54.

Cippi from J. F. Borghouts, "Witchcraft, Magic, and Divination in Ancient Egypt," in Jack M. Sasson, editor, *Civilizations of the Ancient Near East*, New York: Scribner's, 1995, vol. 3, p. 1782.

Astrology and Babylon from Burton and Grandy, p. 43.

Brodie-Innes quote from Richard Cavendish, "Magic," in Richard Cavendish, ed., *Man, Myth, & Magic: The Illustrated Encyclopedia of Mythology, Religion, and the Unknown,* New York: Marshall Cavendish, 1995, vol. 11, p. 1583.

Newton on gravity cited in Burton and Grandy, p. 41.

Crowley quote from Richard Cavendish, "Magic," in Richard Cavendish, ed., *Man, Myth, & Magic: The Illustrated Encyclopedia of Mythology, Religion, and the Unknown,* New York: Marshall Cavendish, 1995, vol. 11, p. 1583.

Clarke quote from Arthur C. Clarke, *Report on Planet Three and Other Speculations,* New York: Harper & Row, 1972, p. 139.

Chaper 3: Stars, Spells, and the Philosopher's Stone
Charlemagne's death from Dan Burton and David Grandy, *Magic, Mystery, and Science: The Occult in Western Civilization,* Bloomington: Indiana University Press, 2004, p. 43.

Anne Boleyn and Witchcraft Statute from Eric Maple, "Love Magic," in Richard Cavendish, ed., *Man, Myth, & Magic: The Illustrated Encyclopedia of Mythology, Religion, and the Unknown,* New York: Marshall Cavendish, 1995, vol. 11, p. 1560.

Hermes Trismegistus from Burton and Grandy, pp. 56–58.

St. Germain and James Price from Burton and Grandy, pp. 84–85.

"Wild brew" from Burton and Grandy, p. 58.

Chapter 4: Wizards and Sorcerers
Urban VIII from Richard Cavendish, "Magic," in Richard Cavendish, ed., *Man, Myth, & Magic: The Illustrated Encyclopedia of Mythology, Religion, and the Unknown,* New York: Marshall Cavendish, 1995, vol. 11, p. 1582 and Brendan Dooley, Introduction, *Morandi's Last Prophecy and the End of Renaissance Politics,* Princeton, NJ: Princeton University Press, 2002, online at http://press.princeton.edu/chapters/i7229.html and "Glimpses of Church History," online at goacom.org/overseas-digest/Religion/Church%20History/1600-1700.html and "Tommaso Campanella" in *Stanford Encyclopedia of Philosophy,* online at http://plato.stanford.edu/entries/campanella/#Year.html0

Gigli quote from Brendan Dooley, Introduction, *Morandi's Last Prophecy and the End of Renaissance Politics,* Princeton, NJ: Princeton University Press, 2002, online at http://press.princeton.edu/chapters/i7229.html

Paracelsus quote from Richard Cavendish, "Magic," in Richard Cavendish, ed., *Man, Myth, & Magic: The Illustrated Encyclopedia of Mythology, Religion, and the Unknown*, New York: Marshall Cavendish, 1995, vol. 11, p. 1583.

Levi's four rules and Levi quote from Richard Cavendish, "Magic," in Richard Cavendish, ed., *Man, Myth, & Magic: The Illustrated Encyclopedia of Mythology, Religion, and the Unknown*, New York: Marshall Cavendish, 1995, vol. 11, p. 1580.

SPR on Blavatsky from Dan Burton and David Grandy, *Magic, Mystery, and Science: The Occult in Western Civilization*, Bloomington: Indiana University Press, 2004, p. 213.

Wicker quote from Christine Wicker, *Not in Kansas Anymore: A Curious Tale of How Magic Is Transforming America*, New York: HarperSanFrancisco, 2005, p. 50.

What Do You Think?

Tutankhamen curse from *Egypt: Land of the Pharaohs*, Alexandria, VA: Time-Life Books, 1992, pp. 119–134 and Dan Burton and David Grandy, *Magic, Mystery, and Science: The Occult in Western Civilization*, Bloomington: Indiana University Press, 2004, pp. 31–33 and David Keys, "Curse of the Mummy Invented by Victorian Writers," online at www.egyptvoyager.com/articles_curseofmummy.html and James Randi, "Tut, curse of king," in *Encyclopedia of Claims, Frauds, and Hoaxes of the Occult and Supernatural*, online at www.randi.org/encyclopedia/Tut,%20Curse%20of%20King.html

Winlock and curse from Thomas Hoving, *Tutankhamun: The Untold Story*, New York: Simon and Schuster, 1978, p. 229.

Real Egyptian curses from J. H. Borghouts, "Witchcraft, Magic, and Divination in Ancient Egypt," in Jack M. Sasson, ed., *Civilizations of the Ancient Near East*, New York: Scribner's, 1995, vol. 3, p. 1771 and Hoving, pp. 226–228 and "Curse of King Tut's Tomb," online at www.mummytombs.com/egypt/kingtut.html

About the Author

Rebecca Stefoff's many books for young readers cover a wide range of topics in science, history, and literature. Scary stories and vampire movies are among her favorite entertainments. As a member of CSICOP (the Committee for the Scientific Investigation of Claims of the Paranormal), Stefoff supports a thoughtful, research-based approach to supernatural and paranormal subjects. She lives in Portland, Oregon.